NUTRiBULLET
RECIPE BOOK

NUTRiBULLET
RECIPE BOOK

The New Nutribullet Recipe Book with Fat Burning
Smoothies for Weight Loss, Energy and Good Health -
Works with Nutribullet and Other Personal Blenders

Edition: 3

SHERYL JENSEN

TABLE OF CONTENTS

THE DOCTOR OF THE FUTURE IS HERE!.................................9
BREAKFAST ENERGY BLASTS................................... 15
   Green Mellow Blast 15
   Fruits & Seeds Combo 17
   Pineapple Frenzie Blast.................................. 18
   Slimming Apple Carrot..................................... 19
   Mixed Green Fruta 20
   Raspy Avocado Blast.. 21
   Banana Bell Jingle 22
   Swiss Grape Ribbon 23
   Green Fruity Fiesta.. 24
   Strawberry Avocado Split................................. 25
   Creamy Green Chunk 26
   Green Strawberry Zest..................................... 27
EVERYDAY HEALTHY BLASTS.............................. 28
   Raspy Kale Fix 28
   Apple Beet Fusion Blast................................... 30
   Mango Papaya Blast 31
   Raspy Dandy Blast.. 32
   Peach Banza Blast... 33
   Gingery Nutri Bliss 34
   Spinach Cucumber Blast.................................. 35
   Pineapple Kale Blast 36
   Blueberry Fiddles 37
   Crunchy Pineapple Blast................................... 38

Orange Carrot Blast.. 39

Blueberry Greens Blast.. 40

Mixed Fruit Blast... 41

Tropicana Peak Blast... 42

Honeydew Mint Blast... 43

Peachy Blueberry Blast 44

Spiced Leafy Greens Blast..................................... 45

GREEN DETOX BLASTS 46

Green Pear Blast.. 46

Avocado Cream Blast... 48

Cucumber Cooler Blast.. 49

Fruity Combo Blast 50

Zesty Green Blast.. 51

Sweet & Creamy Blast... 52

Celery Kiwi Blast... 53

Green Vegetable Blast 54

Festive Apple Blast.. 55

Creamy Green Blast... 56

Zesty Fruit Blast 57

Cucumber & Greens Blast...................................... 58

HIGH ENERGY BLASTS 59

Gingery Kiwi Blast... 59

Banana Pear Blast... 61

Orange Carrot Blast... 62

Green Pineapple Blast... 63

Blueberry Banana Blast... 64

Tutti Fruity Blast... 65

Pomegranate Strawberry Blast...66

Greek Pumpkin Blast..67

Raspberry Spinach Blast..68

Coco Mango Blast...69

WEIGHT LOSS BLASTS...70

Silky Grape Blast..70

Apple Cranberry Blast...72

Vegetable Medley Blast...73

Apple & Kale Blast...74

Orange Berry Blast...75

Peachy Apricot Blast..76

Green Cucumber Blast...77

Orange Strawberry Blast...78

Nutty Pear & Apple Blast..79

Blackberry Vanilla Blast..80

Blueberry Lettuce Blast...81

Kiwi & Kale Blast..82

PROTEIN POWER BLASTS..83

Creamy Strawberry Blast..83

Almond Mango Blast..85

Cucumber Cooler Blast..86

Icy Berries & Greens Blast..87

Mango Banana Blast...88

Cherry & Broccoli Blast...89

Watermelon Cantaloupe Blast..90

Creamy Banana Blast...91

Mango Carrot Blast..92

Fruity Cocobana Blast..93

Banana Kale Blast...94

Citrus Berry Blast 95

SMART BLASTS FOR KIDS...96

Tropicana Swizzle Blast 96

Creamy Banana Blast 98

Mango Spinach Blast 99

Moo Moo Strawberry Blast 100

Apple Parfait Blast...101

Kale Berry Blast..102

Creamy Cocoa Blast...103

Vanilla Almond Blast 104

Pineapple Cherry Blast 105

Chocolaty Banana Blast...106

CHEERS—TO LONG LIFE!..107

THE DOCTOR OF THE FUTURE IS HERE!

*"The doctor of the future will no longer treat the human frame with drugs, but rather will cure and prevent disease with nutrition." –**Thomas Edison, Renowned American Inventor***

Unquestionably, we're living in exciting times! And if you own a *Nutribullet* you couldn't be more excited. Many health enthusiasts consider the *Nutribullet* an absolutely essential part of a healthy lifestyle. And it truly is. The world's first nutrition extractor is here—the doctor of the future! The *Nutribullet* is the first nutrition extractor of its kind. Millions of *Nutribullet* owners have come to agree with its manufacturers about its high performance, ease of use and its absolutely amazing nutrient extraction technique for maximizing the nutrition and flavor of foods. Hence, the *Nutribullet* is well celebrated as the perfect kitchen-mate for making some of the most nutrient-dense smoothies, soups, sauces and more. It's definitely a must-have for a healthy kitchen and a healthy lifestyle.

As you may already know, smoothie variations with the *Nutribullet* are often referred to as "Nutriblasts". This is because, unlike a regular blender or juicer which does partial nutrient extraction, the *Nutribullet* is totally different. Instead, it fully extracts food nutrients by uniquely breaking down and grinding the cell walls of food for optimum nutrient release and absorption into our body. Thereby, every time you drink one of these wholefood smoothies, there is an incredible unleashing of a "nutrient-packed blast" also known as a "nutriblast" into our system. And that in itself is simply astounding! It is an open door to good health. Additionally, some of the acclaimed health benefits of drinking "nutriblast" smoothies include: reversing signs of aging, boosting the immune system, increasing energy levels and ultimately increasing longevity and overall good health.

The reality is that good health is one of life's greatest treasures. There's hardly much that we can do without it. However, in a busy world where processed foods are increasingly available, eating healthy is a serious challenge. Wouldn't you agree? A processed food temptation lurks around almost every corner, thus our healthy existence is seriously threatened. For this reason, this *Nutribullet* smoothie book presents you with melt-in-your-mouth smoothies that will provide your body with essential nutrients for good health and long life. Within seconds, you can enjoy a freshly extracted smoothie blast and give your body the natural nourishment that it needs.

Now, it isn't hard to whip up a delicious smoothie blast in just a few minutes. However, always combining the right smoothie ingredients for your health can seem really daunting. For this reason, this isn't just another *Nutribullet* recipe book. There's much more to the perfect *Nutribullet* smoothie than throwing a bunch of ingredients together and calling it a "blast". Instead, these blasts are created with a healthy lifestyle at heart. By drinking just one of these specially formulated smoothie blasts daily, you will begin to feel more energized, you may naturally lose weight and your body will become more resistant to illnesses. And who wouldn't want that? In fact, all that goodness is the perfect foundation for living a happy and fulfilled life. Furthermore, this *Nutribullet Recipe Book* welcomes you to a world of delicious and easy smoothie blasts that are all conveniently calorie counted with local ingredient measurements for both US and UK nutriblasters.

NUTRIBULLET SMOOTHIES—A NUTRITIONAL POWERHOUSE!

In this era of great craze over supplements, there are millions of people regularly consuming expensive pills in the name of nutrition. Despite all this, there's nothing like the kind of nutrition you can get from a freshly made Nutribullet smoothie with the right fruits and vegetables. Medical research has already proven that all the nutrients that the human body requires are present in balanced quantities of fruits and vegetables. Hence, a diet that includes regular consumption of these Nutribullet smoothies can potentially provide all the nutritional needs of the body.

Now, the overall benefit of drinking these Nutribullet smoothies isn't rocket science. Results come about from the *Nutribullet's* optimum nutrient release power for healthy cell regeneration. Healthy cell regeneration is cyclical in the body and becomes necessary for a vibrant and functional body. So, whether we are aware or not, our food choices play a vital role in the vibrancy of newly regenerated cells.

Here's the bottom line. These smoothie blasts have been used for weight loss and to ward off degenerative diseases such as the Big "C" (cancer), diabetes, hypertension, heart disease, obesity and more. This works because the right combination of fruits and vegetables will produce an alkalizing effect in the body. This alkalinity in the body further helps to provide protection against acidity and also propels the body to produce more hemoglobin in the blood. *Hemoglobin* is a kind of red blood cell protein which is responsible for transporting oxygen from the lungs to the cells throughout the body. Hence, without adequate hemoglobin levels, the body does not have enough energy to perform optimally. Feelings of low energy levels, extreme tiredness and fainting spells are common signs of low hemoglobin levels. Ultimately, drinking these nutritional smoothie blasts is a great way of combating low hemoglobin levels and thus improving your overall health.

NUTRIBULLET SMOOTHIES—THE WEIGHT LOSS FOOD

Apart from the *Nutribullet's* nutritional benefits towards general good health, it is also a weightwatcher's friend. Many nutriblasters have experienced moderate to significant weight loss by increasing their consumption of fruits and vegetables with these *Nutribullet* smoothies. This is because most fruits and vegetables are significantly high in natural nutrients, high in fiber, low in calories and low in fat—all essential components for weight loss.

Ideally, all the smoothies in this book can be used as a part of a successful weight loss regime. For accelerated weight loss, smoothies with a good balance of fruits and vegetables works best and these can be found throughout the book. Additionally, using a smoothie as a meal replacement is a common and proven weight loss approach. Another common weight loss approach involves a smoothie fasting day. Typically, a smoothie fasting day (days) should include mainly *Green Detox Blasts* or other water-based smoothies. Apart from drinking up to 8 cups (64 ounces/2 liters) of smoothies each fasting day, food consumption on smoothie fasting days should be limited to fruits, nuts, vegetables and water. Bear in mind that it is a good idea to consult your doctor before starting any weight loss or fasting regime, especially for persons with known health issues.

Interestingly, you don't necessarily have to fast or do meal replacements to lose weight with these smoothies. This is because natural weight loss will usually occur with regular consumption. It is however important that you do not consume your smoothies with a meal. For maintaining an ideal weight, it is best to have your smoothies at least 30-45 minutes after a meal. This is to avoid too many added calories and to allow your system adequate time for proper digestion. So, instead of focusing on fasting or dieting, just enjoy these smoothies for the joy of it. Eventually, you should begin to see the results of improved health.

NUTRIBULLET BASICS

Mastering the art of using your *Nutribullet* doesn't require culinary expertise. Almost anyone can use it like a pro. If you are already familiar with successfully using the *Nutribullet*, you may skip this section and go straight to the recipes. The accompanying instruction manual with your Nutribullet has very comprehensive guidelines for using it successfully. However, here follows some essential reminders that you may also find handy. Let's do the basics:

- Your Nutribullet doesn't work like a slow cooker and thus requires more monitoring. It must be properly monitored to ensure that all is well during the extraction process from start to finish.

- Always remember to unplug your *Nutribullet* whenever you're not using it.

- Wash your Nutribullet according to the manufacturer's instruction either immediately after extracting or as soon as possible. It is better to clean sooner than later.

- For super quick and easy Nutribullet breakfast smoothies, you may prepare your ingredients overnight.

- Always remember the Max Line rule: when loading liquid into your *Nutribullet*, never let your liquid pass the Max Line. Doing this will help to prevent unnecessary leakages and messes. For thicker smoothies, use less liquid and for thinner smoothies use more.

- Do not process your *Nutribullet* smoothies for minutes. A complete extraction process takes only about 40-50 seconds.

- Never put hot liquids or other hot ingredients in your *Nutribullet*.

- Don't let your kids use your *Nutribullet* until you've shown them what to do and you are confident that they can handle it.

- Always add liquid along with your other ingredients. Liquid helps to ensure that things run smoothly.

- If your ingredient is as hard as a rock, don't put it in your *Nutribullet*.

Let's Have A Blast!

With this *Nutribullet Recipe Book* you can use your *Nutribullet* to make nutritious blasts which could help you to stay fit and healthy. So, whether you want to lose some pounds or just simply improve your health, there is a smoothie in this book for everyone. For certain, we all deserve to live happy and fulfilled lives, and drinking these *Nutribullet* smoothies is one of the easiest ways to do just that. Now, go ahead and choose your first smoothie recipe to kick-start or embrace a lifestyle of health and happiness. Let's have a blast!

Tasty Glass of Nutriblast Smoothie!

BREAKFAST ENERGY BLASTS

Green Mellow Blast

Sip your way smarter with this delicious breakfast smoothie. The combination of blueberry and fresh greens also adds a unique taste to this very healthy and fiber-rich smoothie.

MAKES: 1 serving
PREPARATION TIME: 5 minutes

Calories per serving: 249

½ cup (120ml) fat-free Milk

½ cup (120ml) fat-free plain Greek Yogurt

1 cup (144g) fresh Blueberries

½ cup (28g) fresh Baby Greens

2 Medjool Dates, pitted and chopped

2 Ice Cubes

Directions

- Add all the ingredients to the tall cup.
  - Process until smooth.
    - Enjoy your blast.

Fruits & Seeds Combo

This recipe is a super energy boosting combination for a smoothie. This drink will also be a great choice for a high fiber nutritional drink.

MAKES: 1 serving
PREPARATION TIME: 5 minutes

Calories per serving: 364

¾ cup (180ml) Fresh Apple juice

1 Apple, peeled, cored and chopped

½ cup (70g) Blueberries, frozen

1 cup (30g) Fresh Baby Spinach

½ tablespoon Raw Wheat Germ

1 tablespoon Flax Seeds

2 tablespoons Pumpkin Seeds

Stevia, to taste (optional)

2 Ice Cubes

Directions

- Add all the ingredients to the *tall cup*.
  - Process until smooth.
    - Enjoy your blast.

Pineapple Frenzie Blast

The healthy combination of milk, yogurt, pineapple and kale makes this great tasting smoothie very interesting. The addition of protein powder adds an extra nutritional boost to this drink and also promotes appetite control.

MAKES: 1 serving
PREPARATION TIME: 5 minutes

Calories per serving: 315

½ cup (120ml) chilled fat-free Milk

¼ cup (60ml) fat-free plain Greek Yogurt

1 cup (166g) frozen Pineapple chunks

1 cup (67g) fresh Baby Kale

1 scoop Protein Powder, unsweetened

Directions

- Add all the ingredients to the *tall cup.*
- Process until smooth.
- Enjoy your blast.

Slimming Apple Carrot

This is a wonderfully delicious smoothie with powerful health benefits. The addition of fresh lemon juice in this recipe adds a bright and refreshing twist to this drink.

MAKES: 1 serving
PREPARATION TIME: 5 minutes

Calories per serving: 121

¾ cup (180ml) Filtered Water

1 teaspoon Fresh Lemon Juice

1 Green Apple, peeled, cored and chopped

1 small Carrot, peeled and chopped

1 cup (43g) Fresh Baby Kale

Stevia or Preferred Sweetener, to taste (optional)

2 Ice Cubes

Directions

- Add all the ingredients to the *tall cup.* Add water as desired while ensuring that it doesn't pass the *Max Line.*
  - Process until smooth.
  - Enjoy your blast.

Mixed Green Fruta

This is a super healthy green smoothie with fresh juices which will boost your energy levels and immune system.

MAKES: 1 serving
PREPARATION TIME: 5 minutes

Calories per serving: 163

½ cup (120ml) Fresh Orange juice

¼ cup (60ml) Fresh Carrot juice

½ Green Apple, peeled, cored and chopped

½ small Banana, peeled, sliced and frozen

2 Broccoli Florets, chopped

½ cup (20g) Fresh Baby Kale

2 Ice Cubes

Directions

- Add all the ingredients to the *tall cup.*
- Process until smooth.
- Enjoy your blast.

Raspy Avocado Blast

A delicious and a truly eye-opening smoothie for the morning! The avocado in this recipe provides a naturally creamy texture to this fresh and satisfying smoothie.

MAKES: 1 serving
PREPARATION TIME: 5 minutes

Calories per serving: 357

½ cup (120ml) fresh Raspberry juice

½ cup (120ml) chilled fresh Orange juice

½ cup (62g) fresh Raspberries

1 slice (100g) Avocado, peeled and chopped

2 Ice Cubes

Directions

- Add all the ingredients to the *tall cup.*
- Process until smooth.
- Enjoy your blast.

Banana Bell Jingle

This is among one of the best smoothies prepared with green bell pepper. The use of banana in this drink adds a naturally sweet complementary flavor.

MAKES: 1 serving
PREPARATION TIME: 5 minutes

Calories per serving: 105

¾ cup (180ml) Filtered Water

¼ cup (10g) Green Cabbage, chopped

½ small Green Bell Pepper, seeded and chopped

1 small Ripe Banana, peeled and sliced

4 Ice Cubes

Directions

- Add all the ingredients to the *tall cup.*
- Process until smooth.
- Enjoy your blast.

Swiss Grape Ribbon

This is a simple and healthy recipe for a delicious green smoothie. The grapes in this drink add an extra nutritional kick to this healthy smoothie.

MAKES: 1 serving
PREPARATION TIME: 5 minutes

Calories per serving: 176

¾ cup (180ml) Filtered Water

½ teaspoon Fresh Lemon juice

1cup (90g) Seedless Green Grapes

1 cup (35g) Fresh Swiss Chard, trimmed and chopped

1 tablespoon Maple Syrup or preferred sweetener (optional)

2 Ice Cubes

Directions

- Add all the ingredients to the *tall cup.*
- Process until smooth.
- Enjoy your blast.

Green Fruity Fiesta

This is a delicious combination for a green smoothie. You can enjoy this drink with a nutritional serving of mixed fruits and fresh spinach.

MAKES: 1 serving
PREPARATION TIME: 5 minutes

Calories per serving: 351

---

1 cup (240ml) Soy Milk

½ Ripe Banana, peeled and sliced

½ cup (80g) Pineapple Chunks, frozen

½ cup (80g) Peach, peeled, cored, chopped and frozen

1½ cup (45g) Fresh Baby Spinach

½ scoop Unsweetened Protein Powder

½ tablespoon Ground Flaxseeds

Maple Syrup or preferred sweetener (optional)

2 Ice Cubes

Directions

- Add all the ingredients to the *tall cup.*
- Process until smooth.
- Enjoy your blast.

Strawberry Avocado Split

This is one of the perfect ways to enjoy strawberries when they are in season. In this smoothie the strawberries are blended with milk, yogurt, chia seeds and avocado to make a delicious nutrient dense drink.

MAKES: 1 serving
PREPARATION TIME: 5 minutes

Calories per serving: 322

¼ cup (60ml) Fat-Free Milk

¾ cup (180ml) Fat-Free Plain Yogurt

1½ cup (216g) Strawberries, frozen

1 slice (100g) Avocado, peeled and sliced

½ tablespoon Chia Seeds

2 Ice Cubes

Directions

- Add all the ingredients to the *tall cup.*
- Process until smooth.
- Enjoy your blast.

Creamy Green Chunk

This is one of the best energy boosting smoothies for the whole family. The avocado in this recipe adds a natural creaminess to this green vegetable smoothie.

MAKES: 1 serving
PREPARATION TIME: 5 minutes

Calories per serving: 420

¾ cup (180ml) Coconut Milk Kefir

1 cup (70g) Fresh Kale, trimmed and chopped

½ small Avocado, peeled, pitted and chopped

½ tablespoon Extra-virgin Coconut Oil

1 tablespoons Honey or preferred sweetener (optional)

2 Ice Cubes

Directions

- Add all the ingredients to the *tall cup.*
- Process until smooth.
- Enjoy your blast.

Green Strawberry Zest

Enjoy this healthy collard greens smoothie with a balanced blend of fruits. Chia seeds are added as an extra nutritional boost while the lemon juice gives it a zesty flavor.

MAKES: 1 serving
PREPARATION TIME: 5 minutes

Calories per serving: 194

---

1 cup (240ml) Filtered Water

½ tablespoon fresh Lemon Juice

1 large ripe Banana, peeled and sliced

1 cup (144g) ripe Strawberries, hulled

1 cup (45g) Collard Greens, stems removed and chopped

1 tablespoon organic Chia Seeds

Directions

- Add all the ingredients to the *tall cup.*
- Process until smooth.
- Enjoy your blast.

EVERYDAY HEALTHY BLASTS

Raspy Kale Fix

Kale and other ingredients are combined to give a great flavor to this drink. With the coconut water and pineapple chunks, there is no need to crave for added sugar in this smoothie. This is a healthy and delicious smoothie. Enjoy.

MAKES: 1 serving
PREPARATION TIME: 5 minutes

Calories per serving: 261

1 cup (240ml) Unsweetened Organic Coconut Water

1 cup (67g) fresh Kale, trimmed and torn

½ cup (80g) fresh Pineapple Chunks

1 cup (144g) Raspberries Berries

1 tablespoon Ground Flaxseeds

Directions

- Add all the ingredients to the *tall cup.*
- Process until smooth.
- Enjoy your blast.

Note: For variation and added nutritional boost, you may also add a tablespoon of organic extra-virgin coconut oil to this recipe.

Apple Beet Fusion Blast

Create a vibrant, red colored smoothie with this fantastic smoothie recipe. This incredibly rich smoothie is packed with body cleansing and immune boosting ingredients that will help to keep your body healthy.

MAKES: 1 serving
PREPARATION TIME: 5 minutes

Calories per serving: 239

---

1 cup (240ml) fresh Orange juice

1 small Apple, peeled, cored and sliced

1 small Beet, trimmed, peeled and chopped

½ small Carrot, peeled and chopped

¼ teaspoon Fresh Ginger, chopped

Stevia or preferred sweetener, to taste (optional)

2 Ice Cubes

Directions

- Add all the ingredients to the *tall cup.*
- Process until smooth.
- Enjoy your blast.

Mango Papaya Blast

Bring the taste of the tropics into your house with this tasty blend of tropical fruits with milk and some protein-rich yogurt. This delicious smoothie may be enjoyed by the whole family.

MAKES: 1 serving
PREPARATION TIME: 5 minutes

Calories per serving: 246

½ cup (180ml) fat-free Milk

½ cup (180ml) fat-free plain Greek Yogurt

½ cup (94g) Mango, frozen, peeled, pitted and chopped

½ cup (70g) Papaya, frozen, peeled and chopped

1 cup (67g) fresh Kale, trimmed and chopped

Stevia or preferred sweetener, to taste (optional)

2 Ice Cubes

Directions

- Add all the ingredients to the *tall cup*.
- Process until smooth.
- Enjoy your blast.

Raspy Dandy Blast

Coconut helps to bring out the unique flavor in this delicious smoothie. The combination with raspberries, banana, chia seeds and milk makes a healthy and fulfilling drink which is bursting with energy.

MAKES: 1 serving
PREPARATION TIME: 5 minutes

Calories per serving: 320

---

1 cup (240ml) chilled fat-free Milk

1 cup (124g) fresh Raspberries

1 small Banana, peeled and sliced

1 cup (30g) fresh Baby Spinach

2 tablespoons Coconut, shredded

1 tablespoon Chia Seeds

Directions

- Add all the ingredients to the *tall cup.*
- Process until smooth.
- Enjoy your blast.

Note: *For variation and added nutritional boost, you may also add a tablespoon of organic extra-virgin coconut oil to this recipe.*

Peach Banza Blast

Peach und banana is being brilliantly combined with orange and lime juice to make a wonderfully refreshing smoothie. This drink will become an easy favorite when fresh peaches are in season.

MAKES: 1 serving
PREPARATION TIME: 5 minutes

Calories per serving: 250

---

1 cup (240ml) fresh Orange juice

½ tablespoon fresh Lime juice

1 cup (55g) Romaine Lettuce, torn

1 medium Peach, pitted and chopped

1 small Banana, peeled and sliced

2 Ice Cubes

Directions

- Add all the ingredients to the *tall cup.*
- Process until smooth.
- Enjoy your blast.

Gingery Nutri Bliss

Enjoy the added flavor and anti-inflammatory benefits of ginger in this smoothie. With a mix of kale, mango, and watermelon there is added nutrients and antioxidants. Your taste buds and body will love this drink!

MAKES: 1 serving
PREPARATION TIME: 5 minutes

Calories per serving: 267

¾ cup (180ml) Filtered Water

1 cup (67g) fresh Kale, trimmed and torn

1 Ripe Mango, peeled, pitted and chopped

½ cup (76g) Watermelon, seeded and chopped

1 teaspoon fresh Ginger, chopped

2 Ice Cubes (optional)

Directions

- Add all the ingredients to the *tall cup.*
- Process until smooth.
- Enjoy your blast.

Spinach Cucumber Blast

Throw together this green smoothie when you want to increase your intake of greens! This drink is wonderfully healthy, and it is packed with balanced nutrients. The addition of ginger adds powerful antioxidant benefits and a lovely flavor to this smoothie.

MAKES: 1 serving
PREPARATION TIME: 5 minutes

Calories per serving: 394

---

1 cup (240ml) fat-free Milk

1 Avocado, peeled, pitted and chopped

1 cup (30g) fresh Baby Spinach

1 small Cucumber, peeled and chopped

¼ teaspoon fresh Ginger, chopped

Stevia or preferred sweetener, to taste (optional)

2 Ice Cubes

Directions

- Add all the ingredients to the *tall cup.*
- Process until smooth.
- Enjoy your blast.

Pineapple Kale Blast

You can prepare this nutrient-packed smoothie for your family at breakfast or for snack time. The combination of pineapple, kale and banana ensures that this smoothie is nutritionally balanced.

MAKES: 1 serving
PREPARATION TIME: 5 minutes

Calories per serving: 195

---

1 cup (240ml) chilled organic Coconut Water

1 cup (166g) fresh Pineapple Chunks

1 cup (67g) fresh Kale, trimmed and chopped

½ small Banana, peeled and sliced

2 Ice Cubes

Directions

- Add all the ingredients to the *tall cup.*
- Process until smooth.
- Enjoy your blast.

Blueberry Fiddles

There's nothing like adding healthy greens to your smoothies and not tasting it! Romaine lettuce is that healthy greens that does just that. Enjoy this neutral tasting smoothie any time of day.

MAKES: 1 serving
PREPARATION TIME: 5 minutes

1 cup (240ml) Filtered Water

1 cup (144g) fresh Blueberries

1 ripe Pear, seeded and chopped

1 cup (55g) Romaine Lettuce, torn

Directions

- Add all the ingredients to the *tall cup.*
- Process until smooth.
- Enjoy your blast.

Crunchy Pineapple Blast

Enjoy this wonderful and nutritious smoothie treat for the whole family anytime of the day. This healthy and delicious smoothie may become a favorite among your family and friends.

MAKES: 1 serving
PREPARATION TIME: 5 minutes

Calories per serving: 253

---

1 cup (240ml) chilled filtered Water

½ tablespoon fresh Lime juice

½ cup (46g) seedless Green Grapes

½ cup (83g) Pineapple chunks

1 cup (30g) fresh Spinach

2 Medjool Dates, pitted and chopped

2 tablespoons Cashew nuts

Directions

- Add all the ingredients to the *tall cup.*
- Process until smooth.
- Enjoy your blast.

Orange Carrot Blast

Beta Carotene, vitamin A, C and E are some of the nutritional benefits of this smoothie. This nice combination of carrots and the fresh juices of orange and pineapple, delivers a super healthy and refreshing drink.

MAKES: 1 serving
PREPARATION TIME: 5 minutes

Calories per serving: 216

¼ cup (120ml) fresh Orange juice

½ cup (120ml) fresh Pineapple juice

½ cup (120ml) fat-free plain Greek Yogurt

1 cup (112g) Carrots, peeled and chopped

1 cup (35g) Fresh Swiss Chard, trimmed and chopped

2 Ice Cubes

Directions

- Add all the ingredients to the *tall cup.*
- Process until smooth.
- Enjoy your blast.

Blueberry Greens Blast

Add fresh baby greens and blueberries to your diet with this delicious smoothie that is packed with vitamins, nutrients and antioxidants that will aid in keeping your body healthy. The addition of banana also ensures that this drink is a great source of energy.

MAKES: 1 serving
PREPARATION TIME: 5 minutes

Calories per serving: 254

½ cup (120ml) chilled fresh Orange juice

½ cup (120ml) fat-free plain Greek Yogurt

¼ cup (38g) Blueberries, frozen

1 small Banana, peeled and sliced

1 cup (55g) fresh Baby Greens

¼ teaspoon Vanilla Extract

Directions

- Add all the ingredients to the *tall cup.*
- Process until smooth.
- Enjoy your blast.

Mixed Fruit Blast

If you love fresh pears during the pear season, then this is a recipe for you. This recipe combines pear with grapes and kale to deliver an interesting and delicious taste.

MAKES: 1 serving
PREPARATION TIME: 5 minutes

Calories per serving: 287

---

1 tablespoon fresh Lime juice

1 cup (240ml) fat-free plain Greek Yogurt

1 Pear, peeled, cored and sliced

¼ cup (23g) seedless Red Grapes

1 cup (67g) fresh Baby Kale

Stevia or preferred sweetener, to taste (optional)

2 Ice Cubes

Water

Directions

■ Add all the ingredients to the tall cup. Add water as desired while ensuring that it doesn't pass the *Max Line.*

■ Process until smooth.

■ Enjoy your blast.

Tropicana Peak Blast

Papaya, mango and pineapple can add a very tropical twist to your smoothie repertoire. This delicious recipe, with the addition of fresh orange juice and yogurt, makes a refreshing smoothie that is also very healthy.

MAKES: 1 serving
PREPARATION TIME: 5 minutes

Calories per serving: 339

½ cup (120ml) fresh Orange juice

½ cup (120ml) fat-free plain Greek Yogurt

1 cup (67g) fresh Kale, trimmed and chopped

½ cup (70g) Papaya, peeled and chopped

½ cup (94g) Mango, peeled, pitted and chopped

1 cup (166g) Pineapple Chunks

2 Ice Cubes

Directions

- Add all the ingredients to the *tall cup.*
- Process until smooth.
- Enjoy your blast.

Honeydew Mint Blast

When you crave a refreshing drink on a hot day, this smoothie will hit the spot. The combination of fresh lime juice and mint leaves makes this honeydew and banana smoothie unbelievably refreshing.

MAKES: 1 serving
PREPARATION TIME: 5 minutes

Calories per serving: 163

¾ cup (180ml) filtered Water

½ tablespoon fresh Lime juice

1 cup (152g) Honeydew Melon

1 small Banana, peeled and sliced

1 cup (35g) Fresh Swiss Chard, trimmed and chopped

1 tablespoon fresh Mint leaves

2 Ice Cubes

Directions

- Add all the ingredients to the *tall cup.*
- Process until smooth.
- Enjoy your blast.

Peachy Blueberry Blast

Enjoy a quick and easy smoothie anytime of the day with this recipe. The mixture of peach and blueberries with almonds ensures that this drink has a great texture, and that it is packed with vitamins and healthy protein.

MAKES: 1 serving
PREPARATION TIME: 5 minutes

Calories per serving: 167

---

1 cup (240ml) chilled Almond Milk

1 fresh Peach, pitted and chopped

½ cup (77g) fresh Blueberries

1 cup (55g) Romaine Lettuce, torn

½ tablespoon Almonds, chopped

¼ teaspoon Vanilla Extract

Directions

- Add all the ingredients to the *tall cup.*
- Process until smooth.
- Enjoy your blast.

***Note:** For variation and added nutritional boost, you may also add a tablespoon of organic extra-virgin coconut oil to this recipe.*

Spiced Leafy Greens Blast

If you like a bit of spice in your food, you will love this smoothie. This vibrant green smoothie is a delicious blend of healthy leafy greens, dates, almond butter and spices.

MAKES: 1 serving
PREPARATION TIME: 5 minutes

Calories per serving: 309

1 cup (240ml) chilled fat-free Milk

1 cup (30g) fresh Baby Spinach

1 cup (67g) fresh Baby Kale

2 Medjool Dates, pitted and chopped

1 tablespoon Almond Butter

1 tablespoon Chia Seeds

Pinch of Ground Cinnamon

Pinch of Ground Cloves

Directions

- Add all the ingredients to the *tall cup.*
  - Process until smooth.
    - Enjoy your blast.

GREEN DETOX BLASTS

Green Pear Blast

This vibrant green smoothie blends the sweetness of pear and banana with one cup of nutrient packed spinach. This is a delicious and nutrient-dense smoothie that is a great option for green smoothie beginners.

MAKES: 1 serving
PREPARATION TIME: 5 minutes

Calories per serving: 180

½ cup (120ml) chilled organic Coconut Water

½ cup (120ml) chilled filtered Water

1 Pear, peeled, cored and sliced

½ small Banana, peeled and sliced

1 cup (30g) fresh Spinach

Directions

■ Add all the ingredients to the *tall cup.*

- Process until smooth.
- Enjoy your blast.

Note: *For variation and added nutritional boost, you may also add a tablespoon of organic extra-virgin coconut oil to this recipe.*

Avocado Cream Blast

Enjoy this healthy and green smoothie which is made without any dairy products. The use of avocado in this recipe makes this smoothie exceptionally creamy.

MAKES: 1 serving
PREPARATION TIME: 5 minutes

Calories per serving: 321

---

1 cup (240 ml) chilled filtered Water

1 large Green Apple, peeled, cored and sliced

1 small Avocado, peeled, pitted and chopped

Stevia or preferred sweetener, to taste (optional)

Directions

- Add all the ingredients to the *tall cup.*
- Process until smooth.
- Enjoy your blast.

Cucumber Cooler Blast

On a hot summer's day, make this refreshing green smoothie and relax! The cucumber and kiwi combine nicely with fresh parsley, and this drink packs a delicious kick from the addition of ginger.

MAKES: 1 serving
PREPARATION TIME: 5 minutes

Calories per serving: 94

---

1 cup (240 ml) chilled filtered Water

1 Kiwi, peeled and chopped

1 small Cucumber, peeled and chopped

1 tablespoon fresh Parsley leaves

¼ teaspoon fresh Ginger, chopped

Directions

- Add all the ingredients to the *tall cup.*
  - Process until smooth.
    - Enjoy your blast.

Fruity Combo Blast

Combine together pear, grapes and fresh kale to make a great tasting and nutritious smoothie. This drink will provide a great source of vitamins C and E to your daily diet.

MAKES: 1 serving
PREPARATION TIME: 5 minutes

Calories per serving: 133

---

1 cup (240ml) filtered Water

½ tablespoon fresh Lime juice

½ small Pear, peeled, cored and chopped

½ cup (46g) seedless Green Grapes

1 cup (56g) fresh Kale, trimmed and chopped

Stevia or preferred sweetener, to taste (optional)

2 Ice Cubes

Directions

- Add all the ingredients to the *tall cup.*
- Process until smooth.
- Enjoy your blast.

Zesty Green Blast

Add this green breakfast smoothie to your repertoire. This drink has a refreshing flavor from the lemon, and the combination with pear, dandelion greens and cucumber makes a delicious smoothie.

MAKES: 1 serving
PREPARATION TIME: 5 minutes

Calories per serving: 150

---

1 cup (240ml) chilled filtered Water

½ tablespoon fresh Lemon juice

1 small Apple, peeled, cored and sliced

1 small Cucumber, peeled and chopped

1 cup (55g) fresh Dandelion Greens, chopped

Stevia or preferred sweetener, to taste (optional)

Directions

- Add all the ingredients to the *tall cup.*
- Process until smooth.
- Enjoy your blast.

Sweet & Creamy Blast

Add the wonderful flavors of grapes, avocado and mustard greens into your life with this delicious and creamy smoothie. This drink is bursting with natural goodness which is beneficial for your body and mind.

MAKES: 1 serving
PREPARATION TIME: 5 minutes

Calories per serving: 336

½ cup (120ml) filtered Water

1 cup (92g) seedless Green Grapes, frozen

½ small Avocado, peeled, pitted and chopped

1 cup (56g) fresh Mustard Greens

Stevia or preferred sweetener, to taste (optional)

2 Ice Cubes

Directions

- Add all the ingredients to the *tall cup.*
- Process until smooth.
- Enjoy your blast.

Celery Kiwi Blast

Create one of the best combinations of green vegetables and fruit with this green smoothie recipe. This combination makes a delicious and very low calorie smoothie.

MAKES: 1 serving
PREPARATION TIME: 5 minutes

Calories per serving: 58

¾ cups (180ml) filtered Water

½ tablespoon fresh Lemon juice

1 small Kiwi, peeled and chopped

1 Celery Stalk, chopped

1 cup (27g) Lettuce, torn

Stevia or preferred sweetener, to taste (optional)

2 Ice Cubes

Directions

- Add all the ingredients to the *tall cup.*
- Process until smooth.
- Enjoy your blast.

Green Vegetable Blast

Get your daily dose of green vegetables any time of day with this delicious green smoothie. This drink is packed with healthy low calorie ingredients and delivers essential nutrients.

MAKES: 1 serving
PREPARATION TIME: 5 minutes

Calories per serving: 26

---

1 cup (240ml) chilled filtered Water

½ cup (15g) fresh Spinach

¼ cup (23g) Broccoli Florets, chopped

¼ cup (18g) Green Cabbage, chopped

½ small Green Bell Pepper, seeded and chopped

Stevia or preferred sweetener, to taste (optional)

Directions

- Add all the ingredients to the *tall cup.*
- Process until smooth.
- Enjoy your blast.

Festive Apple Blast

This recipe is a fresh, easy and delicious way to have healthy ingredients in a smoothie! The vegetables, apple, ginger and coconut water combine nicely to make a really tasty blend.

MAKES: 1 serving
PREPARATION TIME: 5 minutes

Calories per serving: 154

---

1 cup (240ml) organic Coconut Water

½ tablespoon fresh Lemon juice

1 Green Apple, peeled, cored and sliced

1 Celery Stalk, chopped

½ cup (15g) fresh Baby Spinach

½ cup (27g) Lettuce, chopped

¼ teaspoon Fresh Ginger, chopped

Stevia or preferred sweetener, to taste (optional)

2 Ice Cubes

Directions

- Add all the ingredients to the *tall cup.*
  - Process until smooth.
    - Enjoy your blast.

Creamy Green Blast

This combination of interesting ingredients makes a simple yet great tasting smoothie. This smoothie will be appreciated by all family and friends.

MAKES: 1 serving
PREPARATION TIME: 5 minutes

Calories per serving: 354

---

1 cup (240ml) organic Coconut Water

½ Green Apple, peeled, cored and sliced

½ Pear, peeled, cored and sliced

1 small Avocado, peeled, pitted and chopped

½ cup (28g) fresh Baby Kale

Stevia or preferred sweetener, to taste (optional)

2 Ice Cubes

Directions

- Add all the ingredients to the *tall cup.*
- Process until smooth.
- Enjoy your blast.

Zesty Fruit Blast

This recipe makes it easy to meet your daily requirement of healthy nutrients in a fun and delicious way. It is an excellent source of vitamin C, E, and other essential nutrients.

MAKES: 1 serving
PREPARATION TIME: 5 minutes

Calories per serving: 161

---

1 cup (240ml) filtered Water

½ tablespoon fresh Lemon juice

1 Pear, peeled, cored and sliced

1 Kiwi, peeled and chopped

1 cup (56g) fresh Kale, trimmed and chopped

Stevia or preferred sweetener, to taste (optional)

2 Ice Cubes

Directions

- Add all the ingredients to the *tall cup.*
- Process until smooth.
- Enjoy your blast.

Cucumber & Greens Blast

Create a perfect and balanced smoothie for the whole family with this recipe. This smoothie not only provides a healthy dose of vitamins and nutrients in just one glass, it also combines great tasting ingredients.

MAKES: 1 serving
PREPARATION TIME: 5 minutes

Calories per serving: 55

---

1 cup (240ml) filtered Water

½ tablespoon fresh Lime juice

½ small Cucumber, peeled and chopped

1 cup (55g) fresh Dandelion Greens, chopped

1 Celery Stalk, chopped

¼ teaspoon Fresh Ginger, chopped

Stevia or preferred sweetener, to taste (optional)

2 Ice Cubes

Directions

- Add all the ingredients to the *tall cup.*
- Process until smooth.
- Enjoy your blast.

HIGH ENERGY BLASTS

Gingery Kiwi Blast

Enjoy this energetic smoothie which provides a nice start to a summer meal. The ginger adds a wonderful kick to this drink and provides anti-inflammatory benefits.

MAKES: 1 serving
PREPARATION TIME: 5 minutes

Calories per serving: 333

---

1 cup (240ml) fresh Grape juice

½ tablespoon fresh Lime juice

1 Kiwi, peeled and chopped

1 cup (152g) Honeydew Melon, peeled and chopped

1 cup (55g) Romaine Lettuce, torn

¼ teaspoon fresh Ginger, chopped

1 scoop Protein Powder, unsweetened

2 Ice Cubes

Directions

- Add all the ingredients to the *tall cup.*
  - Process until smooth.
    - Enjoy your blast.

Note: *For variation and added nutritional boost, you may also add a tablespoon of organic extra-virgin coconut oil to this recipe.*

Banana Pear Blast

You can power up your mornings or snack times with this fantastic smoothie. All the ingredients of this drink provide a rich source of energy and good nutrition.

MAKES: 1 serving
PREPARATION TIME: 5 minutes

Calories per serving: 307

---

1 cup (240ml) fresh Orange juice

1 Pear, peeled, cored and chopped

1 small Banana, peeled and sliced

1 cup (30g) fresh Spinach leaves, chopped

½ tablespoon ground Flux Seeds

Directions

- Add all the ingredients to the *tall cup.*
- Process until smooth.
- Enjoy your blast.

Orange Carrot Blast

The blending of orange, carrot and hemp seeds provides a great tasting smoothie. This easily prepared drink is packed with vitamin c, beta carotene and helps to promote overall good health.

MAKES: 1 serving
PREPARATION TIME: 5 minutes

Calories per serving: 183

½ cup (240ml) fresh Orange juice

1 Orange, peeled, seeded and sectioned

1 small Carrot, peeled and chopped

½ tablespoon Hemp Seeds

Stevia or preferred sweetener, to taste (optional)

2 Ice Cubes

Directions

- Add all the ingredients to the *tall cup.*
- Process until smooth.
- Enjoy your blast.

Green Pineapple Blast

Treat your family to this wonderfully delicious smoothie. This sweet and tangy drink is like having a glass of sunshine on a very misty day!

MAKES: 1 serving
PREPARATION TIME: 5 minutes

Calories per serving: 205

½ cup (120ml) Almond Milk

¾ cup (124g) fresh Pineapple chunks

1 Orange, peeled, seeded and sectioned

½ cup (34g) fresh Kale, trimmed and chopped

1 teaspoon Chia Seeds

2 Ice Cubes

Directions

■ Add all the ingredients to the *tall cup.*

■ Process until smooth.

■ Enjoy your blast.

Blueberry Banana Blast

Combine together flax seeds, banana, protein powder and blueberries to make a natural energy booster. This smoothie is packed with healthy ingredients and will help you to maintain your energy levels throughout the day.

MAKES: 1 serving
PREPARATION TIME: 5 minutes

Calories per serving: 428

---

1 cup (240ml) chilled fat-free Milk

½ cup (77g) fresh Blueberries

1 small Banana, peeled and sliced

1 cup (56g) fresh Kale, trimmed and chopped

1 tablespoon Hemp Seeds

1 scoop Protein Powder, unsweetened

1 teaspoon Flax Seeds

Directions

- Add all the ingredients to the *tall cup.*
- Process until smooth.
- Enjoy your blast.

Tutti Fruity Blast

This recipe nicely mixes together tarty and sweet fruits to create a very re-freshing and delicious smoothie. Not only does this drink taste great, but it will also provide an energy boost whenever needed.

MAKES: 1 serving
PREPARATION TIME: 5 minutes

Calories per serving: 200

¾ cup (180ml) chilled organic Coconut water

½ tablespoon fresh Lime juice

1 Orange, peeled, seeded and sectioned

½ small Apple, peeled, cored and sliced

¼ cup (92g) seedless Red Grapes

1 cup (35g) Fresh Swiss Chard, trimmed and chopped

1 teaspoon Chia Seeds

Directions

- Add all the ingredients to the *tall cup.*
- Process until smooth.
- Enjoy your blast.

Note: For variation and added nutritional boost, you may also add a table-spoon of organic extra-virgin coconut oil to this recipe.

Pomegranate Strawberry Blast

This delicious and healthy smoothie is made by combining strawberries with pomegranate juice, baby greens, banana, and flax seeds. This smoothie may also be loved by kids, and it will provide a healthy energy boost to support their physical activities.

MAKES: 1 serving
PREPARATION TIME: 5 minutes

Calories per serving: 270

---

1 cup (240ml) chilled Pomegranate juice

1 cup (144g) fresh Strawberries

½ small Banana, peeled and sliced

1 cup (45g) fresh Baby Greens

½ tablespoon Flax Seeds

Directions

- Add all the ingredients to the *tall cup.*
- Process until smooth.
- Enjoy your blast.

Greek Pumpkin Blast

Create a fulfilling and delicious smoothie which has a lovely thick texture from the pumpkin puree. This mouth-watering smoothie is packed with healthful vitamins and is a healthy alternative to regular pumpkin pie.

MAKES: 1 serving
PREPARATION TIME: 5 minutes

Calories per serving: 371

½ cup (120ml) Almond Milk

½ cup (120ml) fat-free plain Greek Yogurt

½ cup (123g) homemade Pumpkin Puree

1 cup (55g) Romaine Lettuce, torn

1 small Banana, frozen

½ teaspoon Pumpkin Pie Spice

1 scoop Protein Powder, unsweetened

Stevia or preferred sweetener, to taste (optional)

Directions

- Add all the ingredients to the *tall cup.*
  - Process until smooth.
    - Enjoy your blast.

Raspberry Spinach Blast

Prepare a special and luscious treat for the whole family with this raspberry smoothie recipe. This drink is delicious and bursting with healthy goodness!

MAKES: 1 serving
PREPARATION TIME: 5 minutes

Calories per serving: 407

---

1 cup (240ml) fat-free Milk

1 cup (124g) fresh Raspberries

1 small Banana, peeled and sliced

½ cup (15g) fresh Baby Spinach

1 scoop Protein Powder, unsweetened

1 teaspoon Flax Oil

2 Ice Cubes

Directions

- Add all the ingredients to the *tall cup.*
- Process until smooth.
- Enjoy your blast.

Coco Mango Blast

Get energized at snack time with this nutritious smoothie which tastes great. This simple recipe is made with mango, banana and nutritious kale.

MAKES: 1 serving
PREPARATION TIME: 5 minutes

Calories per serving: 308

½ cup (120ml) cold organic Coconut water

½ cup (120ml) fat-free plain Greek Yogurt

½ cup (94g) Mango, peeled, pitted and chopped

1 small Banana, peeled and sliced

1 cup (67g) fresh Kale, trimmed and chopped

1 tablespoon Flax Meal

Directions

- Add all the ingredients to the *tall cup.*
- Process until smooth.
- Enjoy your blast.

WEIGHT LOSS BLASTS

Silky Grape Blast

Enjoy this refreshing and flavorful green smoothie on a warm summer day. This drink is packed with grapes and avocado which is low in sugars and ideal as part of a weight loss-friendly diet.

MAKES: 1 serving
PREPARATION TIME: 5 minutes

Calories per serving: 430

---

1 cup (240ml) brewed and cooled Green Tea

1 cup (92g) fresh seedless Green Grapes

1 small Avocado, peeled, pitted and chopped

1 cup (55g) Romaine Lettuce, torn

Stevia or preferred sweetener, to taste (optional)

Directions

- Add all the ingredients to the *tall cup.*
    - Process until smooth.
        - Enjoy your blast.

Apple Cranberry Blast

A health boosting combination of apple, cranberries, broccoli and avocado are present in this smoothie. This drink tastes great and it is a perfect treat for anyone on a diabetic diet.

MAKES: 1 serving
PREPARATION TIME: 5 minutes

Calories per serving: 314

---

1 cup (240ml) chilled filtered Water

1 small Apple, peeled, cored and sliced

¼ cup (28g) fresh Cranberries, pitted

½ cup (78g) Broccoli Florets, chopped

1 small Avocado, peeled, pitted and chopped

Directions

- Add all the ingredients to the *tall cup.*
- Process until smooth.
- Enjoy your blast.

Vegetable Medley Blast

Vegetables and grapes are combined in this smoothie to make a wonderfully delicious drink. You are guaranteed to be amazed by this great tasting and antioxidant-rich smoothie.

MAKES: 1 serving
PREPARATION TIME: 5 minutes

Calories per serving: 179

¾ cup (180ml) Soy Milk

½ cup (46g) seedless Green Grapes

¼ cup (39g) Broccoli Florets, chopped

¼ cup (28g) Carrot, peeled and chopped

½ cup (15g) fresh Baby Spinach

2 Ice Cubes

Directions

- Add all the ingredients to the *tall cup.*
- Process until smooth.
- Enjoy your blast.

Apple & Kale Blast

If you are looking for a mellow low calorie smoothie recipe, then this is the one for you! Apple has been combined with kale, celery, parsley and fresh lemon juice to give this smoothie a fantastically refreshing taste.

MAKES: 1 serving
PREPARATION TIME: 5 minutes

Calories per serving: 134

---

1 cup (240ml) chilled filtered Water

½ tablespoon fresh Lemon juice

1 Green Apple, peeled, cored and chopped

1 Celery Stalk, chopped

1 cup (67g) fresh Kale, trimmed and chopped

1 tablespoon fresh Parsley leaves

Directions

- Add all the ingredients to the tall cup.
- Process until smooth.
- Enjoy your blast.

Orange Berry Blast

Create a one glass meal smoothie with this recipe that is bursting with the flavors of fresh orange and mixed berries. This smoothie is a chilled fruity blend of healthy low glycemic fruits!

MAKES: 1 serving
PREPARATION TIME: 5 minutes

Calories per serving: 324

¾ cup (180ml) fat-free plain Greek Yogurt

1 large Orange, peeled, seeded and sectioned

1 cup (45g) Collard Greens, stems removed and chopped

1½ cups (221g) fresh Mixed Berries

2 Ice Cubes

Water

Directions

- Add all the ingredients to the *tall cup.* Add water as desired while ensuring that it doesn't pass the *Max Line.*
- Process until smooth.
- Enjoy your blast.

Peachy Apricot Blast

Combine together fresh peach and apricot with fresh greens to make this delicious smoothie great for the summertime! This smoothie makes an exotic and delicious drink for everyone.

MAKES: 1 serving
PREPARATION TIME: 5 minutes

Calories per serving: 144

---

1 cup (240ml) Almond Milk

1 Peach, peeled, pitted and chopped

½ cup (78g) Apricots, pitted and chopped

½ cup (27g) fresh Greens

2 Ice Cubes

Directions

- Add all the ingredients to the *tall cup.*
- Process until smooth.
- Enjoy your blast.

Green Cucumber Blast

Energize your day with this healthy and refreshing smoothie. The fresh grapefruit compliments the cucumber and dandelion greens nicely, and this combination with milk makes a deliciously healthy drink.

MAKES: 1 serving
PREPARATION TIME: 5 minutes

Calories per serving: 189

½ cup (120ml) fat-free Milk

1 large Grapefruit, peeled, seeded and sectioned

½ cup (28g) fresh Dandelion Greens

½ small Cucumber, peeled and chopped

1 Celery Stalk, chopped

2 Ice Cubes

Directions

- Add all the ingredients to the *tall cup*.
- Process until smooth.
- Enjoy your blast.

Orange Strawberry Blast

Boost your vitamin C intake with this strawberry, orange and spinach smoothie. You will be surprised at how tasty this drink turns out to be and you'll love the flavor from the orange.

MAKES: 1 serving
PREPARATION TIME: 5 minutes

Calories per serving: 176

½ cup (120ml) Almond Milk

½ cup (120ml) fat-free plain Greek Yogurt

½ small Orange, peeled, seeded and sectioned

1 cup (144g) fresh Strawberries, hulled and sliced

1 cup (30g) fresh Baby Spinach

2 Ice Cubes

Directions

- Add all the ingredients to the *tall cup.*
- Process until smooth.
- Enjoy your blast.

Nutty Pear & Apple Blast

If you love the taste of almonds, you will love this smoothie. Packed with almonds and healthy fruits, this delicious smoothie is among the best choices to complement a balanced diet.

MAKES: 1 serving
PREPARATION TIME: 5 minutes

Calories per serving: 344

1 cup (240ml) fat-free Milk

1 medium Pear, peeled, cored and sliced

1 medium Apple, peeled, cored and sliced

1 cup (35g) Fresh Swiss Chard, trimmed and chopped

2 tablespoons Almonds, chopped

¼ teaspoon Vanilla Extract

2 Ice Cubes

Directions

- Add all the ingredients to the *tall cup.*
  - Process until smooth.
    - Enjoy your blast.

Blackberry Vanilla Blast

Make the most of blackberry season with this wonderful blackberry smoothie recipe. The combination with orange juice, milk and vanilla extract makes a truly delicious smoothie that is packed with healthy nutrients, vitamins and fiber.

MAKES: 1 serving
PREPARATION TIME: 5 minutes

Calories per serving: 230

½ cup (120ml) fresh Orange juice

½ cup (120ml) fat-free Milk

1½ cups (221g) fresh Blackberries

1 cup (70g) Fresh Kale, trimmed and chopped

¼ teaspoon Vanilla Extract

2 Ice Cubes

Directions

- Add all the ingredients to the *tall cup.*
- Process until smooth.
- Enjoy your blast.

Note: For variation and added nutritional boost, you may also add a tablespoon of organic extra-virgin coconut oil to this recipe.

Blueberry Lettuce Blast

Lettuce and blueberries combine with cranberry juice and yogurt to make a healthy and delightful smoothie. This recipe is perfect for anyone who wants a pleasant-tasting low sugar drink.

MAKES: 1 serving
PREPARATION TIME: 5 minutes

Calories per serving: 190

½ cup (120ml) fresh Cranberry juice

½ cup (120ml) fat-free plain Greek Yogurt

1 cup (144g) fresh Blueberries

1 cup (55g) Romaine Lettuce, chopped

2 Ice Cubes

Directions

- Add all the ingredients to the *tall cup.*
- Process until smooth.
- Enjoy your blast.

Kiwi & Kale Blast

Enjoy a green colored smoothie with this kiwi, kale and spinach combination. The sweet and tart flavor of the kiwi makes this smoothie light and refreshing.

MAKES: 1 serving
PREPARATION TIME: 5 minutes

Calories per serving: 80

---

1 cup (240ml) chilled filtered Water

1 large Kiwi, peeled and chopped

½ cup (34g) fresh Kale, trimmed and chopped

1 cup (30g) fresh Spinach, chopped

Stevia or preferred sweetener, to taste (optional)

2 Ice Cubes

Directions

- Add all the ingredients to the *tall cup.*
- Process until smooth.
- Enjoy your blast.

PROTEIN POWER BLASTS

Creamy Strawberry Blast

*Enjoy this protein-rich and healthy smoothie recipe which blends together
Greek yogurt, milk, fruit and peanut butter.*

MAKES: 1 serving
PREPARATION TIME: 5 minutes

Calories per serving: 429

½ cup (120ml) fat-free Milk

¼ cup (60ml) fat-free plain Greek Yogurt

½ cup (77g) Strawberries, frozen

1 small Banana, frozen

1 cup (45g) Collard Greens, stems removed and chopped

1 tablespoon natural Peanut Butter

1 scoop Protein Powder, unsweetened

¼ teaspoon Vanilla Extract

Directions

- Add all the ingredients to the *tall cup.*
  - Process until smooth.
    - Enjoy your blast.

Almond Mango Blast

Spice up your range of favorite smoothies with this interesting drink which is a combination of some fantastic super foods. The almond milk complements nicely with the vibrant carrot and tropical mango flavors.

MAKES: 1 serving
PREPARATION TIME: 5 minutes

Calories per serving: 429

---

1 cup (240ml) chilled Almond Milk

¾ cup (135g) Mango, peeled, pitted and chopped

½ cup (56g) Carrot, peeled and chopped

1 cup (55g) Romaine Lettuce, torn

1 tablespoon Almond Butter

1 scoop Protein Powder, unsweetened

1 teaspoon Flax Meal

Directions

- Add all the ingredients to the *tall cup.*
- Process until smooth.
- Enjoy your blast.

Cucumber Cooler Blast

Throw together this excellent smoothie in a few minutes and create a drink that may be loved by the whole family. This high in protein and nutrient rich smoothie may quickly become a firm favorite for all who taste it.

MAKES: 1 serving
PREPARATION TIME: 5 minutes

Calories per serving: 382

---

1 cup (240ml) chilled organic Coconut Water

1 small Pear, peeled, cored and sliced

1 small Cucumber, peeled and chopped

2 tablespoons Cashew nuts, chopped

1 scoop Protein Powder, unsweetened

¼ teaspoon Vanilla Extract

Stevia or preferred sweetener, to taste (optional)

Directions

- Add all the ingredients to the *tall cup.*
- Process until smooth.
- Enjoy your blast.

Icy Berries & Greens Blast

Create a smoothie for your whole family that is both nutritious and refreshing. This drink is loaded with the healthy taste and texture of berries and greens.

MAKES: 1 serving
PREPARATION TIME: 5 minutes

Calories per serving: 435

---

1 cup (240ml) fresh Pomegranate juice

1 cup (144g) fresh Mixed Berries

1 cup (55g) fresh Mixed Greens

1 cup (55g) Romaine Lettuce

1 Medjool Date, pitted and chopped

1 tablespoon Flax Seeds

1 scoop Protein Powder, unsweetened

2 Ice Cubes

Directions

- Add all the ingredients to the *tall cup.*
- Process until smooth.
- Enjoy your blast.

Mango Banana Blast

Mango and banana are blended with coconut water and protein-rich yogurt in this delicious smoothie recipe. Flax seed gives this smoothie a boost of healthy omega-3 nutrients and fiber.

MAKES: 1 serving
PREPARATION TIME: 5 minutes

Calories per serving: 415

½ cup (120ml) chilled organic Coconut Water

½ cup (120ml) fat-free plain Greek Yogurt

½ cup (94g) Mango, peeled, pitted and chopped

1 small Banana, peeled and sliced

1 cup (30g) Fresh Baby Spinach

1 tablespoon Flax Seeds

1 scoop Protein Powder, unsweetened

Directions

- Add all the ingredients to the *tall cup.*
- Process until smooth.
- Enjoy your blast.

Cherry & Broccoli Blast

Amaze yourself with this wonderful combination of cherries, broccoli, dates and pomegranate juice. This wonderful smoothie is packed with nutrients, vitamins and fiber. It is as healthy as it is delicious!

MAKES: 1 serving
PREPARATION TIME: 5 minutes

Calories per serving: 466

---

1 cup (240ml) fresh Pomegranate juice

1 cup (225g) fresh Cherries, pitted

½ cup (46g) Broccoli Florets, chopped

1 cup (35g) Fresh Swiss Chard, trimmed and chopped

2 Medjool Dates, pitted and chopped

1 tablespoon Flax Seed Meal

1 scoop Protein Powder, unsweetened

2 Ice Cubes

Directions

- Add all the ingredients to the tall cup.
  - Process until smooth.
    - Enjoy your blast.

Watermelon Cantaloupe Blast

Combine together watermelon and cantaloupe to make a deliciously flavored smoothie. This drink is among the best smoothies for the summer season.

MAKES: 1 serving
PREPARATION TIME: 5 minutes

Calories per serving: 302

¼ cup (60ml) fresh Orange juice

¼ cup (60ml) fat-free plain Greek Yogurt

1 cup (152g) Watermelon, frozen

½ cup (76g) Cantaloupe, peeled and chopped

1 cup (70g) Fresh Kale, trimmed and chopped

1 tablespoon Cacao Powder

1 scoop Protein Powder, unsweetened

Directions

- Add all the ingredients to the *tall cup.*
- Process until smooth.
- Enjoy your blast.

Creamy Banana Blast

Throw together this simple yet delicious smoothie! The banana, dates and peanut butter combine with the milk and yogurt to make an ultra-creamy and delicious smoothie.

MAKES: 1 serving
PREPARATION TIME: 5 minutes

Calories per serving: 458

¾ cup (180ml) chilled fat-free Milk

¼ cup (60ml) fat-free plain Greek Yogurt

1 medium Banana, peeled and sliced

1 cup (55g) Romaine Lettuce, torn

1 Medjool Date, pitted and chopped

1 tablespoon Peanut Butter

½ tablespoon Wheat Germ

1 scoop Protein Powder, unsweetened

Directions

- Add all the ingredients to the *tall cup.*
- Process until smooth.
- Enjoy your blast.

Mango Carrot Blast

This thick and delicious smoothie is also very refreshing. It will also provide a daily boost of vitamins A, C & E, antioxidants and healthy protein.

MAKES: 1 serving
PREPARATION TIME: 5 minutes

Calories per serving: 318

---

1 cup (240ml) brewed and cooled Green Tea

1 cup (187g) Mango, peeled, pitted and chopped

½ cup (56g) Carrots, peeled and chopped

1 cup (45g) Collard Greens, stems removed and chopped

¼ teaspoon Fresh Ginger, chopped

1 tablespoon Chia Seeds

1 scoop Protein Powder, unsweetened

Stevia or preferred sweetener, to taste (optional)

2 Ice Cubes

Directions

- Add all the ingredients to the *tall cup.*
- Process until smooth.
- Enjoy your blast.

Fruity Cocobana Blast

A flavorful combination of fresh pineapple juice, banana and coconut is used in this smoothie. The addition of fresh lime juice adds a refreshingly tangy touch to this smoothie.

MAKES: 1 serving
PREPARATION TIME: 5 minutes

Calories per serving: 342

½ cup (120ml) chilled fresh Pineapple juice

½ tablespoon fresh Lime juice

½ cup (120ml) fat-free plain Greek Yogurt

½ small Banana, peeled and sliced

1 cup (35g) Fresh Swiss Chard, trimmed and chopped

1 tablespoon Coconut, shredded

1 scoop Protein Powder, unsweetened

Directions

- Add all the ingredients to the *tall cup.*
- Process until smooth.
- Enjoy your blast.

Banana Kale Blast

Utilize fresh kale in this recipe to make a wonderful smoothie using this nutri-ent-dense super food ingredient. The fresh apple juice and banana provides a flavorful and refreshing boost to this drink.

MAKES: 1 serving
PREPARATION TIME: 5 minutes

Calories per serving: 346

½ cup (120ml) Almond Milk

½ cup (120ml) fresh Apple juice

1 medium Banana, peeled and sliced

1 cup (67g) fresh Kale, trimmed and chopped

1 scoop Protein Powder, unsweetened

Stevia or preferred sweetener, to taste (optional)

2 Ice Cubes

Directions

- Add all the ingredients to the *tall cup.*
- Process until smooth.
- Enjoy your blast.

Citrus Berry Blast

Relax and enjoy this fulfilling smoothie which is bursting with the flavors of berries, banana and fresh orange juice. This is a naturally delicious and protein packed smoothie!

MAKES: 1 serving
PREPARATION TIME: 5 minutes

Calories per serving: 391

½ cup (120ml) fresh Orange juice

¼ cup (60ml) fat-free plain Greek Yogurt

½ cup (77g) Blueberries, frozen

½ cup (77g) Strawberries, frozen

1 small Banana, peeled and sliced

1 cup (30g) Fresh Baby Spinach

½ tablespoon Wheat Germ

1 scoop Protein Powder, unsweetened

Directions

- Add all the ingredients to the *tall cup.*
- Process until smooth.
- Enjoy your blast.

SMART BLASTS FOR KIDS

Tropicana Swizzle Blast

This is a deliciously fruity smoothie with a hint of creaminess. A topping of shredded coconut adds a wonderful tropical taste to this drink.

MAKES: 1 serving
PREPARATION TIME: 10 minutes

Calories per serving: 322

½ cup (120ml) Fat-free Milk

1 tablespoon Almond Butter

1 cup (187g) Mango Chunks, fresh or frozen

½ cup (83g) Pineapple Chunks, fresh or frozen

½ cup (20g) Fresh Baby Kale

1 tablespoon Coconut Cream

2 Ice Cubes

Directions

- Add all the ingredients to the *tall cup.*
- Process until smooth.
- Enjoy your blast.

Note: For variation and added nutritional boost, you may also add a table-spoon of organic extra-virgin coconut oil to this recipe.

Creamy Banana Blast

This banana smoothie is a great pick for beginners and picky kids. It is deliciously creamy and has a nice flavor from the banana and almond butter with milk. If you want to make this smoothie sweeter, you may add 1-2 Medjool dates.

MAKES: 1 serving
PREPARATION TIME: 10 minutes

Calories per serving: 378

1 cup (240ml) Almond Milk, unsweetened

1 medium Banana, frozen

1 tablespoon Almond Butter

1 cup (55g) Romaine Lettuce, torn

1 scoop Protein Powder, unsweetened

¼ teaspoon Vanilla Extract

Stevia or Honey, to taste (optional)

2 Ice Cubes

Directions

- Add all the ingredients to the *tall cup.*
- Process until smooth.
- Enjoy your blast.

Mango Spinach Blast

Ensure that your child receives their daily requirement of green vegetables by adding fresh baby spinach to this tasty smoothie. This recipe is a blend of sweet mango and spinach, a combination that will delight the taste buds.

MAKES: 1 serving
PREPARATION TIME: 10 minutes

Calories per serving: 253

½ cup (120ml) fat-free Milk

½ cup (120ml) fat-free plain Greek Yogurt

1 cup (187g) Mango, frozen, peeled, pitted and chopped

1 cup (30g) fresh Baby Spinach

Stevia or Honey, to taste (optional)

2 Ice Cubes

Directions

- Add all the ingredients to the *tall cup.*
- Process until smooth.
- Enjoy your blast.

Moo Moo Strawberry Blast

Make a deliciously creamy strawberry smoothie with the addition of almond butter which adds a wonderfully creamy texture. This smoothie adequately provides a host of vitamins and nutrients for kid's health.

MAKES: 1 serving
PREPARATION TIME: 10 minutes

Calories per serving: 498

---

1 cup (240ml) fat-free Milk

1 cup (144g) fresh Strawberries, hulled and sliced

½ cup (18g) Fresh Swiss Chard, trimmed and chopped

2 Medjool Dates, pitted and chopped

2 tablespoons Almond Butter

1 scoop Vanilla Protein Powder, unsweetened

2 Ice Cubes

Directions

■ Add all the ingredients to the *tall cup.*

■ Process until smooth.

■ Enjoy your blast.

Apple Parfait Blast

Combine together apple, banana, fresh apple juice and yogurt to make a healthy and tasty kid-friendly smoothie. Encourage your kids to make this smoothie and to enjoy the health benefits of this healthy blend.

MAKES: 1 serving
PREPARATION TIME: 10 minutes

Calories per serving: 330

½ cup (120ml) chilled fresh Apple juice

½ cup (120ml) fat-free plain Greek Yogurt

1 Apple, peeled, cored and chopped

1 small Banana, peeled and sliced

½ cup (20g) Fresh Baby Kale

Pinch of Ground Cinnamon

Stevia or Honey, to taste (optional)

Directions

- Add all the ingredients to the *tall cup.*
- Process until smooth.
- Enjoy your blast.

Kale Berry Blast

This smoothie is one of the best ways to develop a taste for greens in your kid's diet. This healthy and tasty smoothie may be loved by all kids!

MAKES: 1 serving
PREPARATION TIME: 10 minutes

Calories per serving: 277

---

1 cup (240ml) chilled fat-free Milk

1 cup (144g) fresh Mixed Berries (of your choice)

1 small Banana, peeled and sliced

½ cup (34g) fresh Baby Kale

Stevia or Honey, to taste (optional)

Directions

- Add all the ingredients to the *tall cup.*
- Process until smooth.
- Enjoy your blast.

Note: For variation and added nutritional boost, you may also add a tablespoon of organic extra-virgin coconut oil to this recipe.

Creamy Cocoa Blast

This is a recipe that will be well received by kids who love chocolate. It is a delicious choice with added benefits from the essential vitamins, fiber and minerals.

MAKES: 1 serving
PREPARATION TIME: 10 minutes

Calories per serving: 445

½ cup (120ml) chilled fat-free Milk

½ cup (120ml) plain Greek Yogurt, fat-free

2 tablespoons Almond Butter

3 Medjool Dates, pitted and chopped

½ cup (20g) Fresh Baby Kale

1 tablespoon Cacao Powder, unsweetened

1 tablespoon Chia Seeds

Stevia or Honey, to taste (optional)

Directions

- Add all the ingredients to the *tall cup*.
- Process until smooth.
- Enjoy your blast.

Vanilla Almond Blast

Enjoy this easy-to-make almond smoothie that is quite different from traditional fruit and vegetable smoothies. This drink is wonderfully delicious and it is also a great healthy option for kids.

MAKES: 1 serving
PREPARATION TIME: 10 minutes

Calories per serving: 270

---

1 cup (240ml) chilled fat-free Milk

¼ cup (24g) Almonds, chopped

2 Medjool Dates, pitted and chopped

½ cup (28g) Romaine Lettuce, torn

¼ teaspoon Vanilla Extract

Directions

- Add all the ingredients to the *tall cup.*
- Process until smooth.
- Enjoy your blast.

Note: For variation and added nutritional boost, you may also add a tablespoon of organic extra-virgin coconut oil to this recipe.

Pineapple Cherry Blast

Create a delicious blend of sweet and tangy flavors all in one irresistible smoothie. This smoothie is a great way to introduce the different flavors to your kids.

MAKES: 1 serving
PREPARATION TIME: 10 minutes

Calories per serving: 210

½ cup (120ml) fat-free Milk

¼ cup (60ml) fat-free plain Greek Yogurt

½ cup (83g) Pineapple Chunks, frozen

½ cup (113g) Cherries, frozen and pitted

½ cup (20g) Fresh Baby Kale

Stevia or Honey, to taste (optional)

Directions

- Add all the ingredients to the *tall cup.*
- Process until smooth.
- Enjoy your blast.

Chocolaty Banana Blast

Cacao powder and banana are a classic combination for a smoothie. This drink is not only easy to make, but it is also a perfect smoothie to support a healthy diet.

MAKES: 1 serving
PREPARATION TIME: 10 minutes

Calories per serving: 165

---

1 cup (240ml) Almond Milk, unsweetened

1 medium Banana, peeled and sliced

½ cup (18g) Fresh Swiss Chard, trimmed and chopped

1 tablespoon Cacao Powder, unsweetened

¼ teaspoon Vanilla Extract

Stevia or Honey, to taste (optional)

2 Ice Cubes

Directions

- Add all the ingredients to the *tall cup.*
- Process until smooth.
- Enjoy your blast.

Note: For variation and added nutritional boost, you may also add a tablespoon of organic extra-virgin coconut oil to this recipe.

CHEERS—TO LONG LIFE!

"By cleansing your body on a regular basis and eliminating as many toxins as possible from your environment, your body can begin to heal itself, prevent disease, and become stronger and more resilient than you ever dreamed possible!" –Dr. Edward Group III

E ver since the early days of making smoothies, we have looked for smoothie makers that will preserve nutrients and conserve time. There's a smoothie maker that provides the best of both words without any compromises. It's the *Nutribullet*, of course—the doctor of the future! Therefore, I'm happy that you've decided to change your life, one smoothie blast at a time. Certainly, the overall health benefits of using the *Nutribullet* to create these healthy and delicious smoothies are endless.

Therefore, the next time you need energy fast, make a blast. With this book, you can enjoy a unique collection of mouthwatering smoothies for your *Nutribullet*. From high energy blasts to smart blasts for kids, this book offers lots of fresh and creative combinations of fruits and vegetables for everyone. Be assured that each glass of superfood blast will bring you much closer to your goal of staying healthy and losing weight.

My journey into living a healthy lifestyle started with my diagnosis of poor memory recall at only twenty-one years old. I had failed to alleviate my problem with prescription drugs, and finally decided to change my eating habits and embrace optimum nutrition. I am really thankful that I am not plagued with those previous health challenges anymore. Thanks to the natural healing power of natural and healthy foods. I am even further grateful that the *Nutribullet* makes it even easier! I strongly believe that if changing my lifestyle has improved my health, it is quite likely that it will improve yours too. For me, the reward of drinking more *Nutribullet* smoothies is priceless.

Moreover, apart from taking the guesswork out of smoothie making, my *Nutribullet* recipes will help you to create easy and nutritious blasts. I really thank you for including my *Nutribullet* smoothies on your journey to a healthier lifestyle. If you have found this book to be helpful, I would appreciate if you would let other readers know about your experience. Cheers—to long life!

Happy Nutriblasting,
Sheryl Jensen

Printed in Great Britain
by Amazon